DUSTY:
Mad or Sad

A book about a Young Mouse and
her Journey with Bipolar Disorder.

BY ANGELA MAE BENCHLEY

WestBow Press books may be ordered through booksellers or by contacting:

WestBow Press
A Division of Thomas Nelson & Zondervan
1663 Liberty Drive
Bloomington, IN 47403
www.westbowpress.com
1 (866) 928-1240

ISBN: 978-1-9736-8574-6 (sc)
ISBN: 978-1-9736-8573-9 (e)

Library of Congress Control Number: 2020902640

Print information available on the last page.

WestBow Press rev. date: 03/11/2020

WESTBOW
PRESS®
A DIVISION OF THOMAS NELSON
& ZONDERVAN

This book is dedicated to my family and friends who have blessed me with their love and support.

In loving memory of my
Aunt Helen Alwood

Once upon a time there lived a family of mice. They called themselves the Purples. These mice were not just regular mice. They could talk and walk on their hind legs.

There was a time when the family was short on food. So everyday the Purples would set out to find food. Sometimes they would go days without food.

Dusty, who was the shade of gray solved their problem for she pretended she was a piece of dust and very carefully collected scraps of food. The other family members would not have gotten away with this for they were too brightly colored.

Dusty was known as their family hero. She had always felt different due to her shade of gray. But now everyone loved the fact she was different.

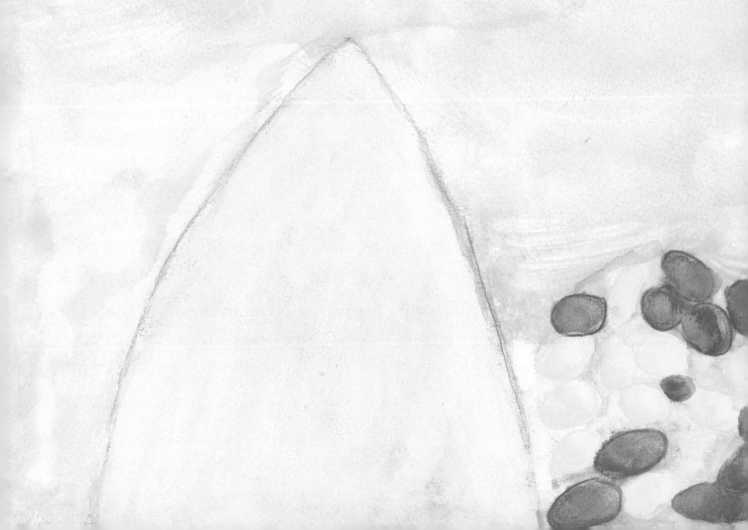

Years later, Dusty's behavior began to change. The other mice never knew what to expect from her. She was very moody. Sometimes she would become very mad. She even didn't care about others' feelings. Dusty would scream loudly. Sometimes she would talk real fast. Her family didn't know what to do.

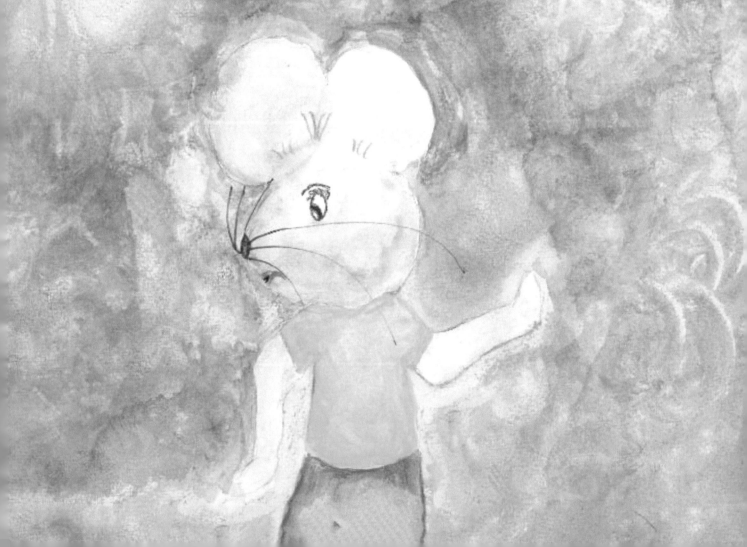

Then there were times when Dusty would spend all her hard earned money she had received from delivering newspapers. She bought things she didn't need. Her room was full of books, vases, jewelry and toys. She even would give away special belongings to her friends and family. She would carefully place each gift in a gift bag ready to deliver.

During these high moods Dusty would come up with grand ideas. She thought she could solve other's problems. Other mice thought she was so helpful they called her an angel.

But then there were times when Dusty would be very sad. She would cry for no reason at all. She would get so upset she couldn't even do her homework or read her favorite books. She talked about not wanting to live anymore. During this mood, Dusty would not even want to see her friends, and would tell them to go away.

There were times when she couldn't sleep and had all kinds of energy. Everyone was impressed with how much work and organizing she did around the house. She would strike up conversations with strangers on the streets and get on the phone with her friends for hours. Her family didn't know what to do with her.

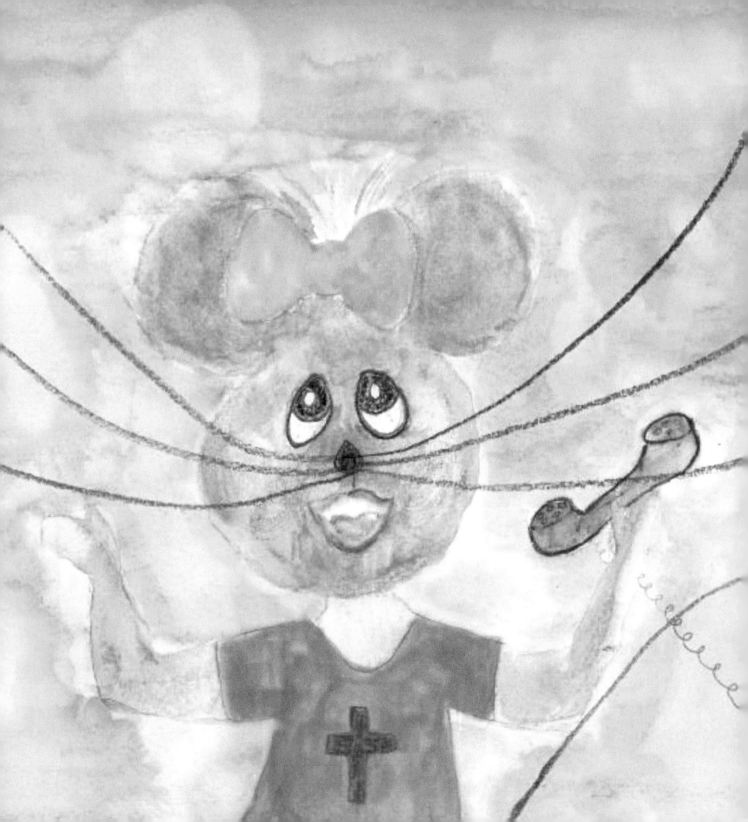

Finally the Purples decided to call a family meeting to discuss Dusty's behavior. Dusty was not acting like herself. They prayed and talked way into the late hours. Dusty was very quiet. Dusty's brother and sister decided they needed to get a doctor to talk to Dusty.

The doctor considered Dusty's mood swings and felt she was suffering from what they called Manic-Depression. The doctor called it an even fancier name: Bipolar Disorder. He explained it is a brain disorder involving mainly two symptoms: mania and major depression.

The good doctor gave Dusty a medicine they called a mood stabilizer. He said the medicine would help her live a balanced life. The mood swings would stop and she would be much happier. He also said she needed to go to bed when her parents told her to.

Sure enough after several weeks Dusty began to feel better. She felt herself coming out of the hole of depression and no longer soaring into the clouds of what they called mania.

She wasn't too sad, too mad or too happy anymore. Dusty finally felt balanced and at peace. She was glad she followed the doctor's orders. The doctor told her this diagnosis was a blessing in disguise for now she could smell the roses. During this time Dusty also felt herself growing closer to God.

The Purples learned everything they could about Bipolar Disorder and discovered it may be genetic. That means other family members have it or could have it.

And sure enough other mice relatives began to tell of their difficult moods. Her aunt and uncle said a mood stabilizer has been helping them for years. They said they also have a therapist who listen to their problems.

Dusty was so glad she was able to get help. Untreated Bipolar Disorder was not any fun. She decided to make a special thank you card for her family, friends and doctor. Dusty said they were heroes too.

Glossary

Bipolar Disorder (or manic depression): a brain disorder involving both mania and/or hypomania usually in addition with depression. Two types of bipolar are bipolar I and bipolar II.

Bipolar I: the classic, florid form of bipolar disorder with the most severe symptoms. Diagnosis is based on having had one or more manic or mixed episodes, usually alternating with major depressive episodes, although some people experience only manic episodes.

Bipolar II: a milder form of bipolar disorder, in which hypomania occurs in place of mania. Hypomanic symptoms may include euphoria that switches to anger and aggression. A hypomanic episode may not include delusions or hallucinations or require hospitalization; however, a depressive episode might.

Clinical Depression: a biologically based form of depression, as opposed to normal grief, unhappiness about a loss, or the blues. Clinical depression involves long-term unrelenting feelings of despair or deadness, and affects cognitive, physical, an/or social functioning.

Mania: a condition that involves extreme changes of moods, thoughts, and feelings; appetite and sleep patterns; energy and activity levels; self-esteem and confidence; and concentration and decision-making abilities.

Mood Stabilizer: a medication used to treat or prevent mania or hypomania. Mood stabilizers can also reduce or prevent depression symptoms.

Resources

Depression and Bipolar Support Alliance
(DBSA), www.DBSAIIiance.org
BPHope.com

Printed in the United States
By Bookmasters